Name________ 

Match the word to the picture. Cut out the word and glue it under the correct picture.

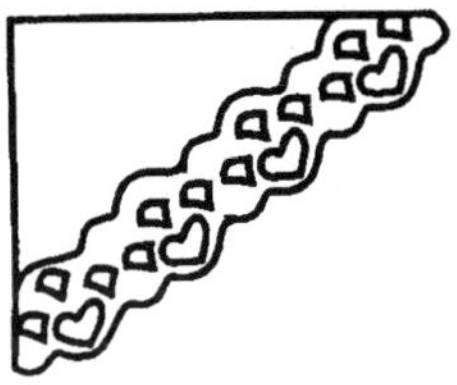

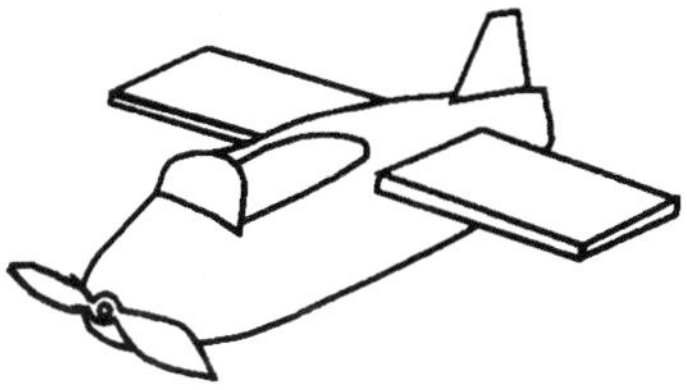

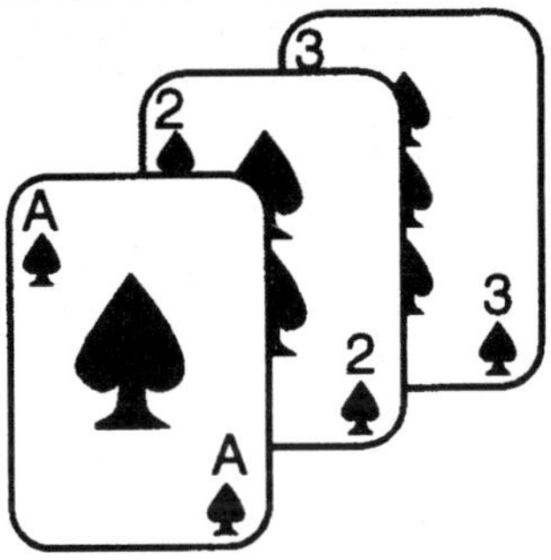

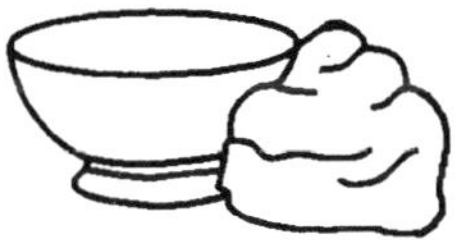

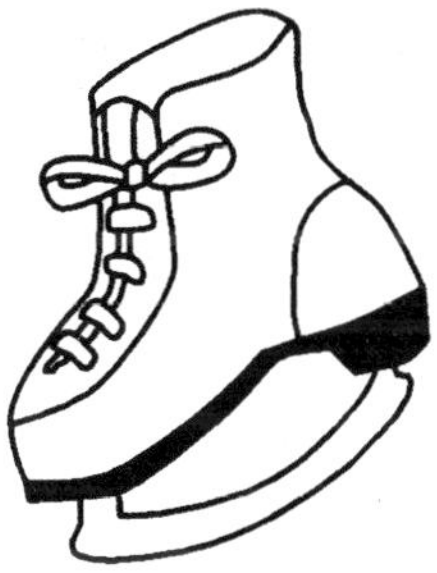

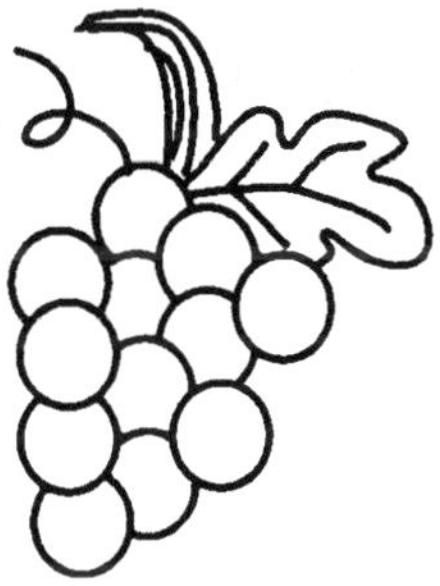

lace

grapes

spade

plane

skate

clay

Name________________________

Fill in the missing letters to make a word that has a long "a" vowel sound.

s ___ i ___	___ ___ ___ l ___	c ___ ___ ___
___ a ___ ___	___ a ___ e	___ ___ ___ y
v ___ ___ e	r ___ ___ ___	___ ___ a ___ e
g ___ ___ d ___	___ ___ i l	t r ___ ___ ___

Name ______________________________

Alphabetize the words at the bottom of the page.

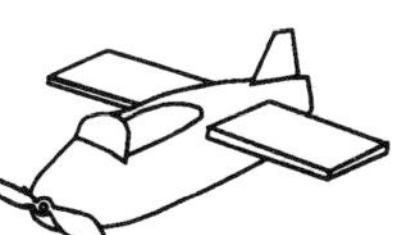

1. ______________________
2. ______________________
3. ______________________
4. ______________________
5. ______________________
6. ______________________
7. ______________________
8. ______________________
9. ______________________
10. ______________________

made	paid
state	crate
quake	spade
main	faint
haste	gave

1. ______________________
2. ______________________
3. ______________________
4. ______________________
5. ______________________
6. ______________________
7. ______________________
8. ______________________
9. ______________________
10. ______________________

plane	sale
maze	make
cape	taste
late	game
trade	wait

Name______________________________

Word Search

The words can be found across, down, diagonally and backwards.

f	m	o	s	t	a	k	e
l	s	t	a	g	e	s	f
a	r	p	i	r	l	t	l
m	y	z	l	a	a	a	a
e	v	s	g	d	b	l	r
c	r	a	n	e	h	e	e
u	d	k	i	c	a	m	e
p	l	a	i	n	t	x	a

Word Bank

grade	plain	flame	sail
stake	stage	bale	vain
stale	crane	came	flare

Table of Contents

Introduction/Purpose

The purpose of putting together the phonics activities in this book is to provide the opportunity for students to see and understand alphabet sound patterns and word families. Phonics Fun Activities, Long Vowels offers both the beginning and developing reader lessons in decoding long vowel sounds. The activities can be used along with the basic instructional materials at the specific grade levels. Other students may also benefit from these activities to review and reinforce the sound patterns and word families.

It is important to remember that people learn at different rates, and in different ways, and that children are little people. Have fun as you work with this material and be aware of the child's readiness level in order to choose and possibly extend appropriate activities.

Information for the Teacher

Instructions for Memory Match:
Pick 2 cards. If they are a match, keep them and draw 2 more. If you do not pick a match, put them back and it is the next player's turn. When there are no more cards available, the winner is the one with the most matches.

Name______________________________

Unscramble the letters making the words in the word bank.

1. e s m a ______________________
2. g a r e ______________________
3. e a k l ______________________
4. e s l a c ______________________
5. c l a p e ______________________
6. i a l n ______________________
7. a g e p ______________________
8. m l f a e ______________________
9. r e d p a ______________________
10. d a i r ______________________

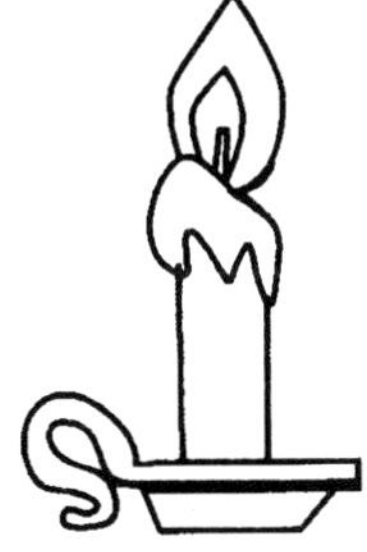

Word Bank			
raid	rage	lake	nail
same	scale	place	drape
	flame	page	

Name ___________________________

Unscramble the sentences. Cut out the words and put them in order to make a sentence. Glue the sentences on a separate piece of paper.

1.

brave	Dave	inside	cave.	the	was	dark

2.

pail.	put	Gail	the	in	the	snail

3.

pay	Ray	the	for	you	clay?	Did

4.

window.	saw	the	crane	Jane	of

plane	the	a	from.

Name________________________________

Write the word that names the picture.

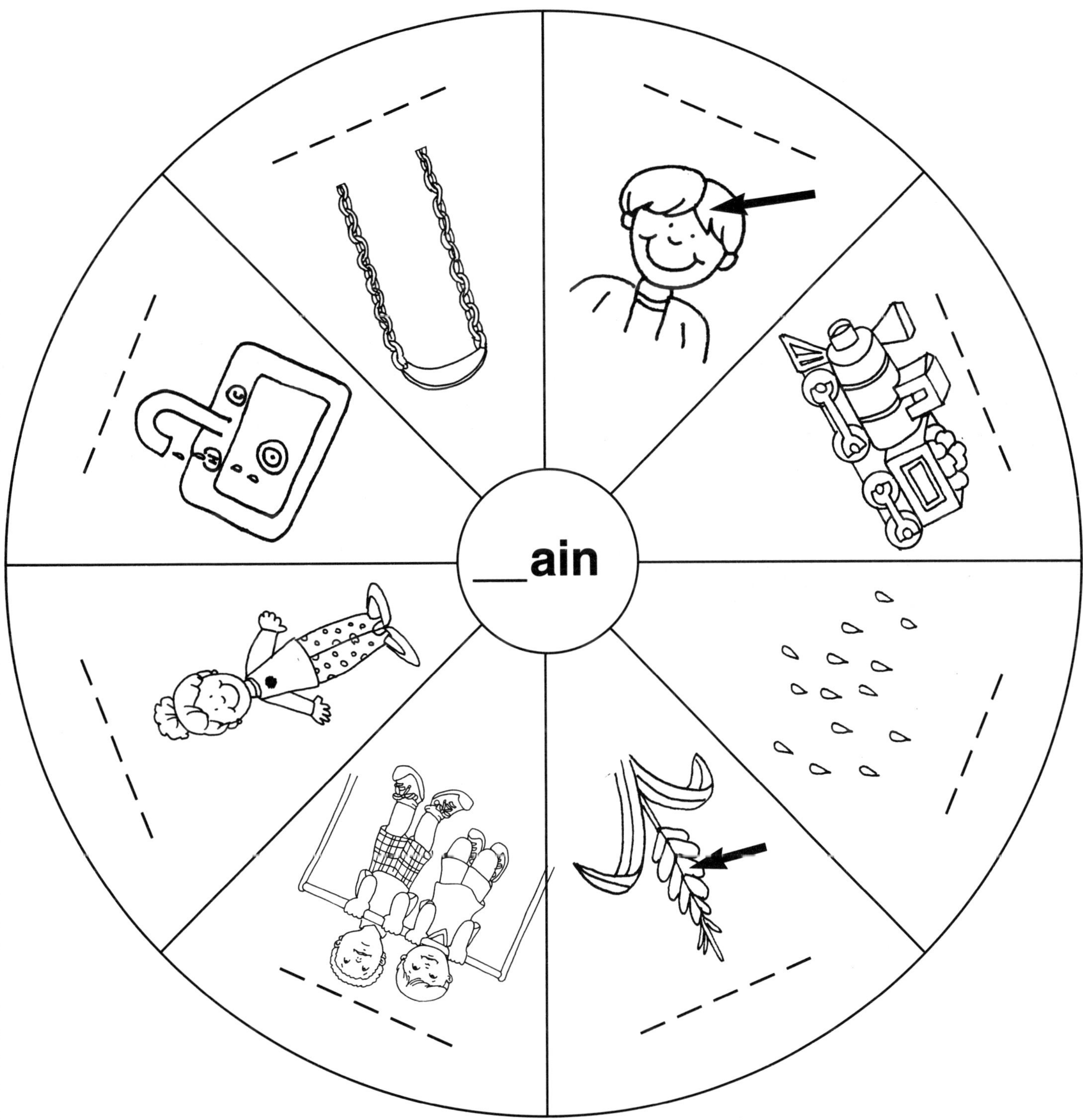

Name________________________

Match the word to its definition. Draw a line from the word to the definition.

1. pail	a. to express approval
2. tame	b. to stay until someone comes
3. praise	c. a bucket
4. wait	d. to change from being wild
5. shake	e. a fruit
6. grape	f. to move up and down or back and forth

Write a sentence using each word.

1. ____
2. ____
3. ____
4. ____
5. ____
6. ____

Name________________________

Write 4 words that rhyme.

Name___________________________

Fill in the missing words.

1. It is nice to sit in the __________ on a hot day.

2. The boys had to __________ the fence during the summer.

3. We took the __________ to go visit Grandma.

4. Paul Bunyan is a tall _________.

5. A __________ is a reptile.

6. Kate woke up at 8:00 and was __________ for school.

7. The girls bought their shoes at a __________.

8. Jake and Nate played a _________ at recess.

Word Bank			
shade	late	train	sale
snake	paint	game	tale

Name____________________________

Sort the words into 2 groups - nouns and verbs. In some cases a word can be both a noun or a verb. Write those words in both groups.

Naming - Nouns	**Action - Verbs**
______________________	______________________
______________________	______________________
______________________	______________________
______________________	______________________
______________________	______________________
______________________	______________________
______________________	______________________
______________________	______________________
______________________	______________________
______________________	______________________

game	laid	snake	spray
take	tail	cage	wade
whale	grain	Spain	paid
vase	jail	pay	trade

Name________________________________

Memory Game

Cut out the word cards. Mix up the cards and place them face down in 3 rows across and 6 rows down. Play "Memory".

quail	frail	jail
tail	sail	snail
nail	trail	hail
quail	frail	jail
tail	sail	snail
nail	trail	hail

Name________________________

Match the word to the picture. Cut out the word and glue it under the correct picture.

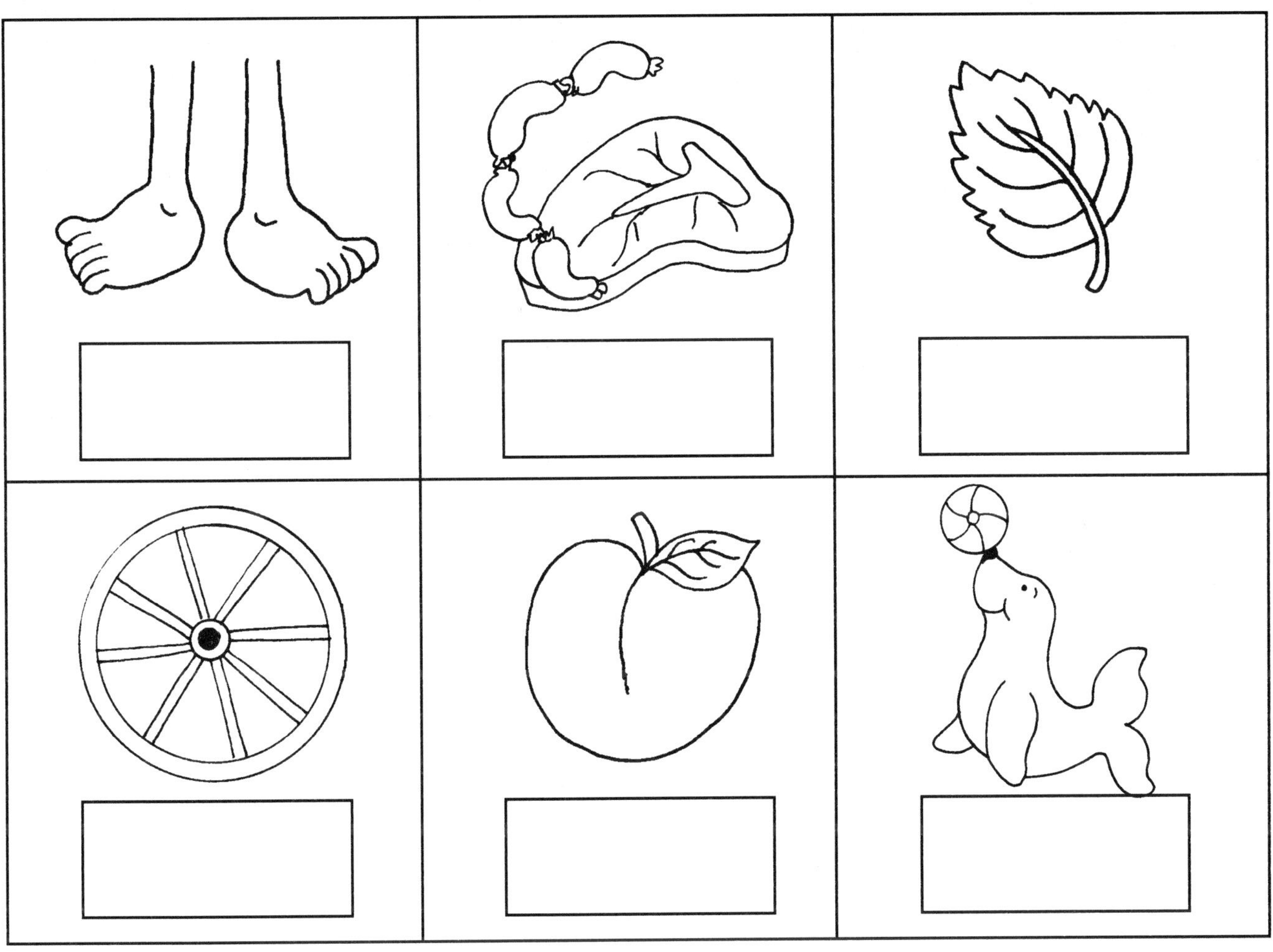

feet

peach

leaf

seal

meat

wheel

Name________________________

Fill in the missing letters to make a word that has a long "e" vowel sound.

c l ___ ___ ___	___ r ___ a t	s ___ r ___ ___ c h
___ e ___ k	l ___ ___ v ___	___ ___ e e z ___
r ___ ___ l	___ e a ___ h	___ e a
s ___ ___ a ___	___ ___ a m	w e ___ p

Name____________________________

Alphabetize the words at the bottom of the page.

1. ____________________
2. ____________________
3. ____________________
4. ____________________
5. ____________________
6. ____________________
7. ____________________
8. ____________________
9. ____________________
10. ____________________

clean
beast
teak
deal
reach
plead
flea
scream
neat
weave

1. ____________________
2. ____________________
3. ____________________
4. ____________________
5. ____________________
6. ____________________
7. ____________________
8. ____________________
9. ____________________
10. ____________________

heat
eat
gleam
zeal
mean
leap
knead
wheat
jeep
queen

Name________________________________

Word Search

The words can be found across, down, up, and backwards.

f	e	e	d	r	e	a	m
c	z	s	t	e	e	l	e
h	o	n	s	g	r	k	e
e	y	e	a	s	t	j	s
e	m	e	c	p	e	e	l
k	a	r	t	e	a	m	e
i	f	g	h	r	p	t	a
b	l	e	e	d	o	j	n

Word Bank

cheek	peel	steel	yeast
lean	tree	team	dream
fee	seem	bleed	green

Name______________________________

Unscramble the letters making the words in the word bank.

1. p w e s e ______________________
2. n l a e ______________________
3. r G k e e ______________________
4. e r c a h ______________________
5. k s e l e ______________________
6. d e p e ______________________
7. n e t e ______________________
8. k u q e a s ______________________
9. t r s e t e ______________________
10. e d e n ______________________

Word Bank			
sleek	teen	Greek	squeak
need	deep	street	reach
	lean	sweep	

Name ______________________________

Unscramble the sentences. Cut out the words and put them in order to make a sentence. Glue the sentences on a separate piece of paper.

1. | bird | loud | squeak | beak. | The | a | its | with | made |
|---|---|---|---|---|---|---|---|---|

2. | steel. | wheel | The | made | was | of |
|---|---|---|---|---|---|

3. | liked | sleep | the | sheep | to | The | jeep. | in |
|---|---|---|---|---|---|---|---|

4. | street. | slipped | His | the | on | the | sleet | in | feet |
|---|---|---|---|---|---|---|---|---|

5. | Allison | tree. | could | up | the | bee | a | see | in |
|---|---|---|---|---|---|---|---|---|

Name________________________

Write the word that names the picture.

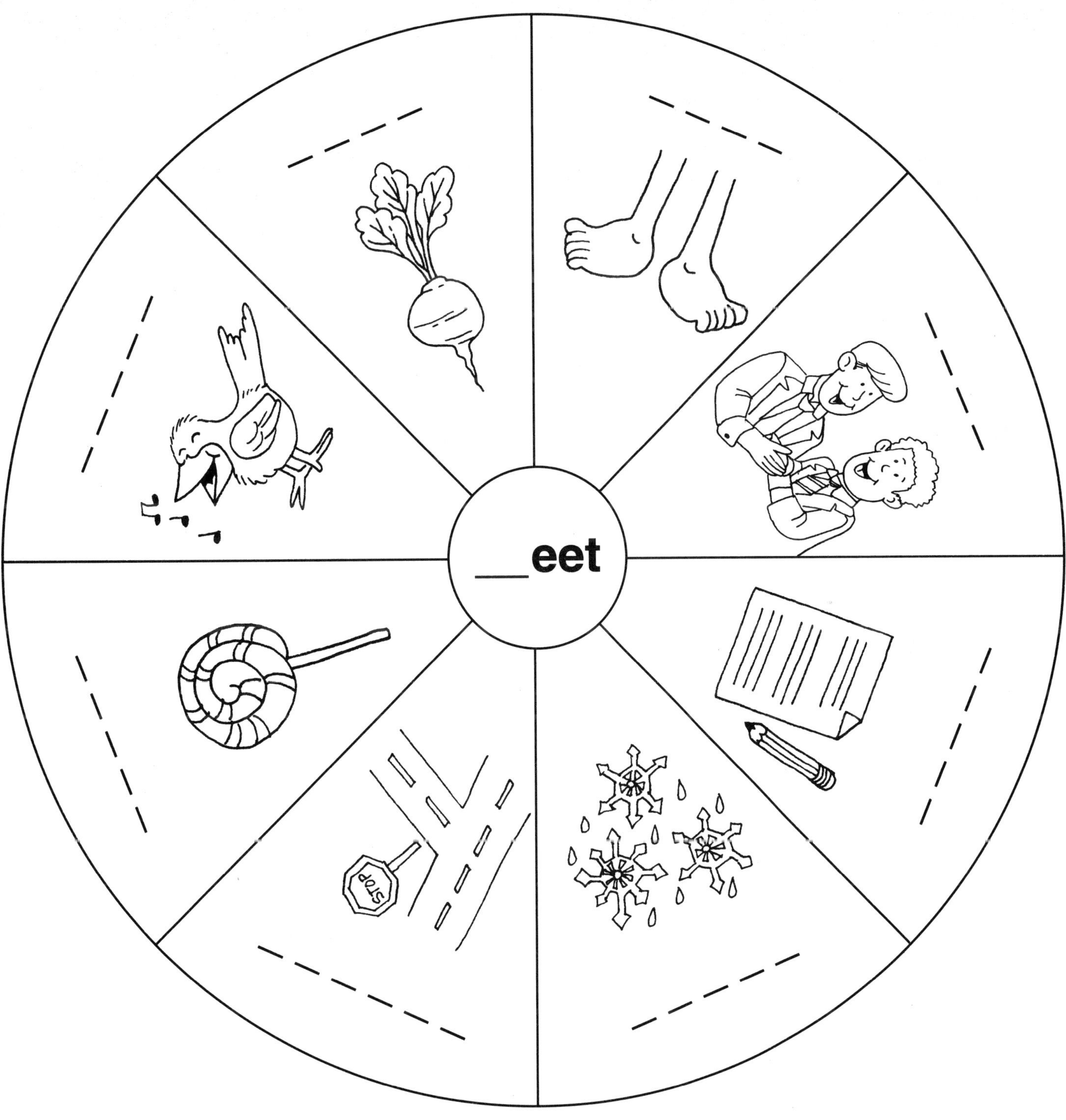

Name____________________________

Match the word to its definition. Draw a line from the word to the definition.

1.	bee	a.	seven days
2.	squeeze	b.	to go fast
3.	week	c.	an insect
4.	speed	d.	to press hard
5.	sleet	e.	a gentle wind
6.	breeze	f.	frozen rain

Write a sentence using each word.

1. ____

2. ____

3. ____

4. ____

5. ____

6. ____

Name______________________________

Write 4 words that rhyme.

Name______________________

Fill in the missing words using the words in the word bank.

1. The boys made a house up in the __________ .

2. Please __________ the garden.

3. The __________ wore a crown.

4. It is fun to __________.

5. __________ softly in the library.

6. A __________ is good for you.

7. The football __________ took a bus to the game.

8. The candy was very __________.

Word Bank			
read	tree	weed	peach
speak	queen	team	sweet

Name ____________________

Sort the words into 2 groups - nouns and verbs. In some cases a word can be both a noun or a verb. Write those words in both groups.

Naming - Nouns	**Action - Verbs**
______________	______________
______________	______________
______________	______________
______________	______________
______________	______________
______________	______________
______________	______________
______________	______________
______________	______________
______________	______________

read	beach	bead	speak
meal	squeak	seal	peach
kneel	weave	cheek	bee
scream	team	queen	bleed

Name_______________________________

Memory Game

Cut out the word cards. Mix up the cards and place them face down in 3 rows across and 6 rows down. Play "Memory".

gleam	lean	heel
bean	freed	creek
plead	squeal	leave
gleam	lean	heel
bean	freed	creek
plead	squeal	leave

Name______________________________

Match the word to the picture. Cut out the word and glue it under the correct picture.

bride	pie
bike	fire
knight	kite

Name______________________________

Fill in the missing letters to make a word that has a long "i" vowel sound.

q ___ i ___ e	___ ___ v e	w ___ ___ t e
s t ___ i ___ e	___ i ___ e	r ___ ___ e
l i ___ ___	___ ___ g h ___	f ___ l ___
t ___ ___ e	w ___ f ___	h ___ ___ h

Name ______________________________

Alphabetize the words at the bottom of the page.

1. ______________________
2. ______________________
3. ______________________
4. ______________________
5. ______________________
6. ______________________
7. ______________________
8. ______________________
9. ______________________
10. ______________________

life
glide
stride
fried
tried

knight
nice
price
bright
while

1. ______________________
2. ______________________
3. ______________________
4. ______________________
5. ______________________
6. ______________________
7. ______________________
8. ______________________
9. ______________________
10. ______________________

pride
tie
sigh
light
mice

rice
wire
fight
crime
vine

Name________________________

Word Search

The words can be found across, down, and diagonally.

b	f	s	p	i	k	e	w
k	r	i	s	e	d	x	r
l	i	f	e	w	h	k	i
f	e	q	u	i	t	e	t
v	d	r	i	v	e	y	e
t	i	d	e	s	i	g	h
i	n	i	n	e	o	v	r
e	a	j	m	w	i	r	e

Word Bank

spike	rise	drive	sigh
nine	write	life	tide
wire	quite	fried	tie

Name______________________________

Unscramble the letters making the words in the word bank.

1. h t i h g ____________________
2. d e l g i ____________________
3. r d e i r ____________________
4. b r i t e ____________________
5. f e n k i ____________________
6. h i w e l ____________________
7. s i e k s ____________________
8. d r e i t ____________________
9. t l i h f g ____________________
10. t i g h l ____________________

Word Bank

knife	glide	tried	flight
tribe	skies	thigh	while
	drier	light	

Name________________________

Unscramble the sentences. Cut out the words and put them in order to make a sentence. Glue the sentences on a separate piece of paper.

1.

light.	The	bright	had	very	a	knight

2.

liked	hike	ride	bike.	his	and	Mike	to

3.

quite	kite	The	was	white	big.

4.

were	bees	live	There	five	the	in	hive.	only

Name________________________

Write the word that names the picture.

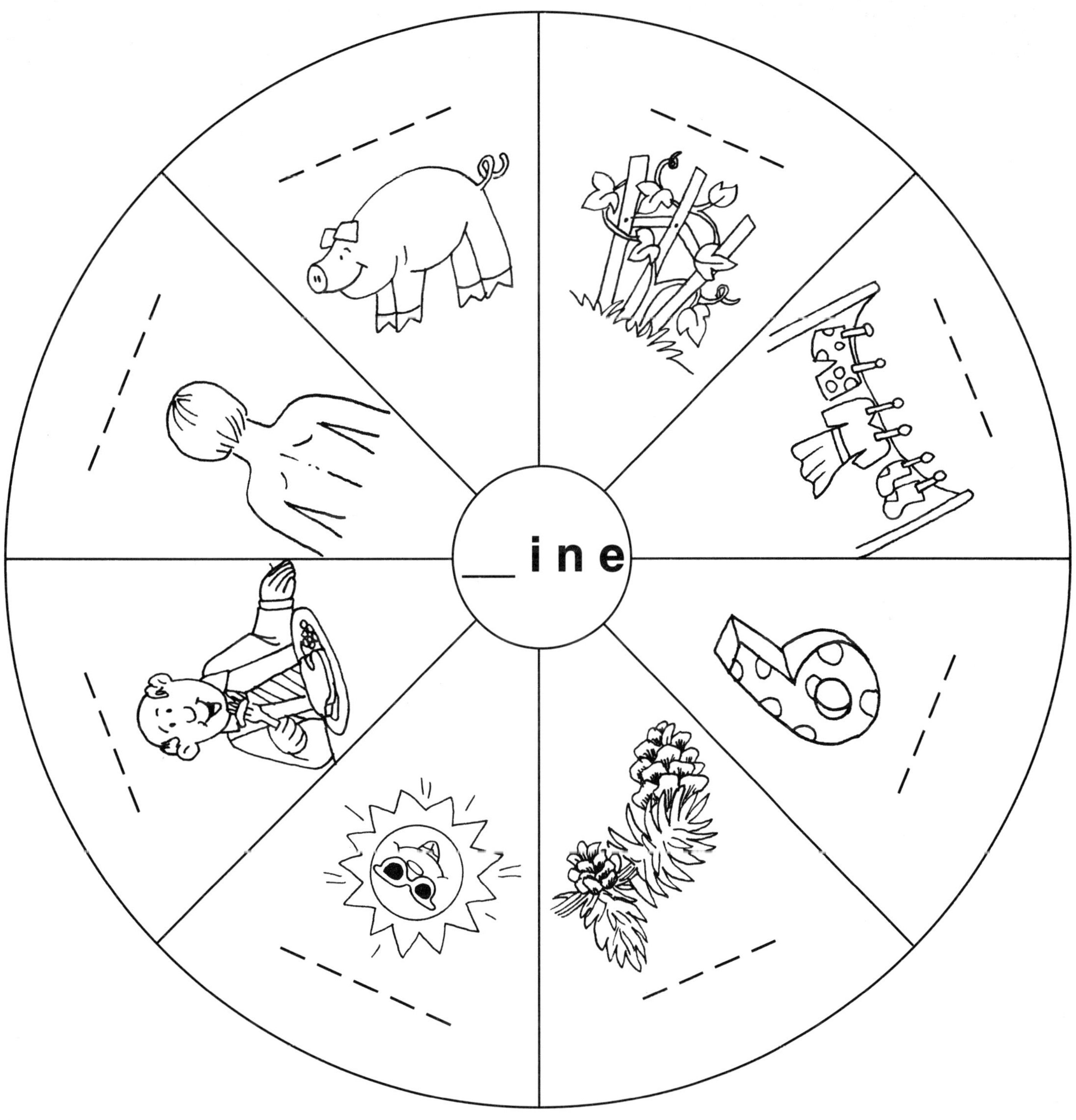

Name________________________

Match the word to its definition. Draw a line from the word to the definition.

1. ripe	a. a heap
2. dime	b. to move smoothly
3. hike	c. ready to eat
4. pile	d. a coin worth ten cents
5. slide	e. a long walk
6. twice	f. two times

Write a sentence using each word.

1. ____
2. ____
3. ____
4. ____
5. ____
6. ____

Name____________________________

Write 4 words that rhyme.

Name___________________________

Fill in the missing words using the words in the word bank.

1. The class __________ go out for recess.

2. The clock on the wall will __________ every hour.

3. A tiger is a __________ animal.

4. The __________ is a river in Egypt.

5. The wind blew the __________ into the tree.

6. Some people __________ to fish.

7. My friend likes to wear __________ colors.

8. __________ is the opposite of left.

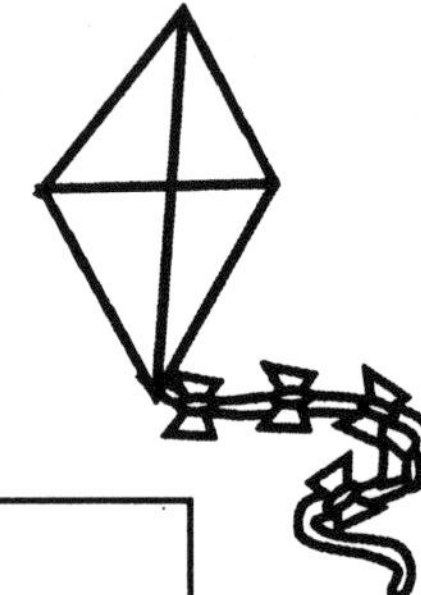

Word Bank			
wild	might	kite	right
Nile	chime	bright	like

Name________________________

Sort the words into 2 groups - nouns and verbs. In some cases a word can be both a noun or a verb. Write those words in both groups.

Naming - Nouns	**Action - Verbs**
______________________	______________________
______________________	______________________
______________________	______________________
______________________	______________________
______________________	______________________
______________________	______________________
______________________	______________________
______________________	______________________
______________________	______________________
______________________	______________________

dime	lice	wipe	knife
cries	glide	pie	strike
write	wife	dine	bike
wipe	child	tile	hire

Name______________________________

Memory Game

Cut out the word cards. Mix up the cards and place them face down in 3 rows across and 6 rows down. Play "Memory".

lime	pike	smile
mild	might	flies
knife	tried	tide
lime	pike	smile
mild	might	flies
knife	tried	tide

Name________________________

Match the word to the picture. Cut out the word and glue it under the correct picture.

toast	phone
toad	crow
hose	smoke

Name______________________________

Fill in the missing letters to make a word that has a long "o" vowel sound.

___ o ___ e	r ___ ___ e	___ o a ___
___ p o ___ e	g ___ ___ b e	___ ___ o n e
s ___ o ___ e	t h ___ s ___	___ ___ o v ___
___ r o ___ ___	w ___ ___ l ___	___ o a ___ ___

Name________________________

Alphabetize the words at the bottom of the page.

1. ________________	1. ________________
2. ________________	2. ________________
3. ________________	3. ________________
4. ________________	4. ________________
5. ________________	5. ________________
6. ________________	6. ________________
7. ________________	7. ________________
8. ________________	8. ________________
9. ________________	9. ________________
10. ________________	10. ________________

loan
coast
float
old
mole
gnome
whole
post
stone
nose

boast
moan
throat
gold
coke
knoll
quote
slope
drove
rope

Name________________________

Word Search

The words can be found across and down.

b	o	l	d	k	j	t	z
l	o	a	d	f	q	h	o
m	w	p	o	l	e	r	n
z	s	r	o	b	e	o	e
h	o	m	e	a	g	a	j
p	a	o	w	s	h	t	o
v	k	d	l	c	y	u	l
h	o	e	b	o	a	s	t

Word Bank

soak	throat	hoe	jolt
load	robe	pole	home
boast	mode	bold	zone

Name_______________________

Unscramble the letters making the words in the word bank.

1. s o e p ______________________

2. n e t o ______________________

3. d o l m ______________________

4. l g o a ______________________

5. l o e r ______________________

6. k e j o ______________________

7. r h o c m e ______________________

8. s r o d e t ______________________

9. s h o e c ______________________

10. n e o r s ______________________

Word Bank			
snore	chose	mold	strode
pose	tone	role	goal
	joke	chrome	

Name________________________

Unscramble the sentences. Cut out the words and put them in order to make a sentence. Glue the sentences on a separate piece of paper.

1.

toast	roast.	We	with	ate	the

2.

fun	It	float	to	moat.	the	in	the	boat	was

3.

his	hoe.	Joe	the	hit	with	toe

4.

gold	She	her	watch.	sold	old,

5.

broke	he	glass	When	at	coke.	joke,

his	he	of	laughed	the

Name____________________________

Write the word that names the picture.

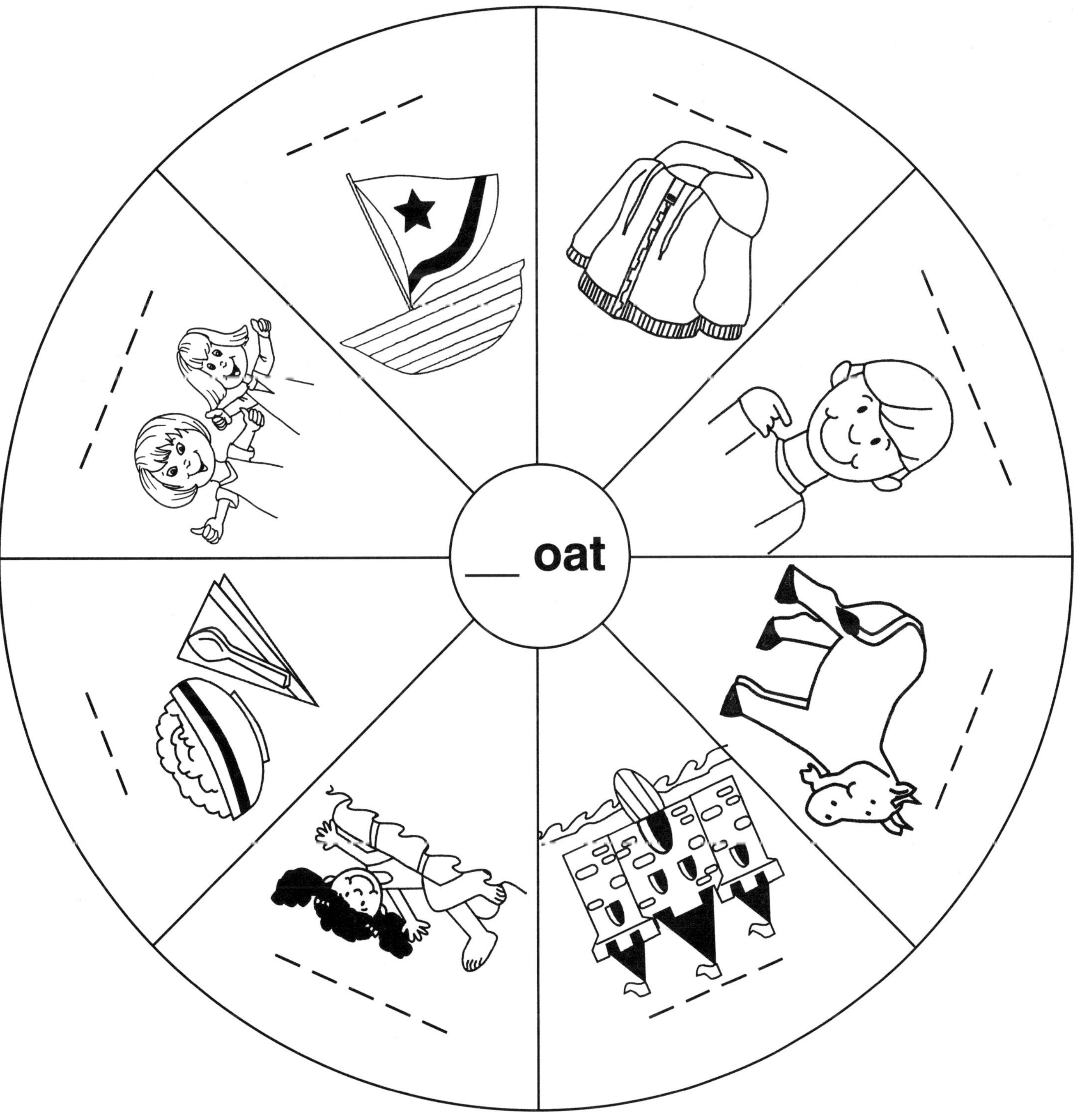

Name____________________________

Match the word to its definition. Draw a line from the word to the definition.

1. boat	a. a young horse
2. chrome	b. the place where you live
3. colt	c. silver metal
4. joke	d. a ship
5. stone	e. something that makes you laugh
6. home	f. rock

Write a sentence using each word.

1. ______________________________
2. ______________________________
3. ______________________________
4. ______________________________
5. ______________________________
6. ______________________________

Name________________________

Write 4 words that rhyme.

Name____________________________

Fill in the missing words using the words in the word bank.

1. He had a cold and a sore __________.

2. The __________ helps the team.

3. Frogs __________ at night.

4. The friends __________ the bus to school.

5. A __________ lives in the woods.

6. The __________ fell out of her pocket.

7. She wore a __________ over her pajamas.

8. The house was __________ down during the tornado.

Word Bank			
rode	robe	throat	coach
blown	rope	doe	croak

Name____________________

Sort the words into 2 groups - nouns and verbs. In some cases a word can be both a noun or a verb. Write those words in both groups.

Naming - Nouns	Action - Verbs
____________________	____________________
____________________	____________________
____________________	____________________
____________________	____________________
____________________	____________________
____________________	____________________
____________________	____________________
____________________	____________________
____________________	____________________
____________________	____________________

float	moan	globe	pole
groan	gold	soak	doe
throat	gnome	colt	hold
stone	rode	poke	boast

Name________________________

Memory Game

Cut out the word cards. Mix up the cards and place them face down in 3 rows across and 6 rows down. Play "Memory".

role	dome	whole
yoke	probe	grown
scope	chose	strode
role	dome	whole
yoke	probe	grown
scope	chose	strode

Name________________________

Match the word to the picture. Cut out the word and glue it under the correct picture.

flute	mule
tube	glue
cube	ruler

Name________________________

Fill in the missing letters to make a word that has a long "u" vowel sound.

___ ___ u m ___	t ___ ___ e	c ___ ___ e
___ u ___	___ ___ u ___ e	___ ___ u e
___ u ___ ___	t ___ ___ e	___ u b ___
___ u ___ e	___ ___ u ___	c h ___ ___ ___

Name____________________________

Alphabetize the words at the bottom of the page.

1. ____________________
2. ____________________
3. ____________________
4. ____________________
5. ____________________
6. ____________________
7. ____________________
8. ____________________
9. ____________________
10. ____________________

cube
true
June
prune
tune
rude
mule
duke
brute
chute

1. ____________________
2. ____________________
3. ____________________
4. ____________________
5. ____________________
6. ____________________
7. ____________________
8. ____________________
9. ____________________
10. ____________________

fuse
brute
plume
dude
cute
due
rule
glue
mute
flute

Name______________________________

Word Search

The words can be found across and down.

j	u	t	e	b	y	d	f	o
r	d	u	e	r	t	a	l	x
u	m	l	f	u	m	e	u	f
d	t	m	u	t	e	t	t	u
e	s	c	u	e	z	u	e	s
p	l	u	m	e	l	c	y	e

Word Bank

fuse	mute	cue	jute
plume	due	rude	flute
cute	fume	brute	

Name____________________________

Unscramble the letters making the words in the word bank.

1. u l e b ______________________
2. t e u j ______________________
3. r e u t ______________________
4. n e u t ______________________
5. l e u r ______________________
6. d d u e ______________________
7. k d e u ______________________
8. l t u f e ______________________
9. b e t u ______________________
10. e t u m ______________________

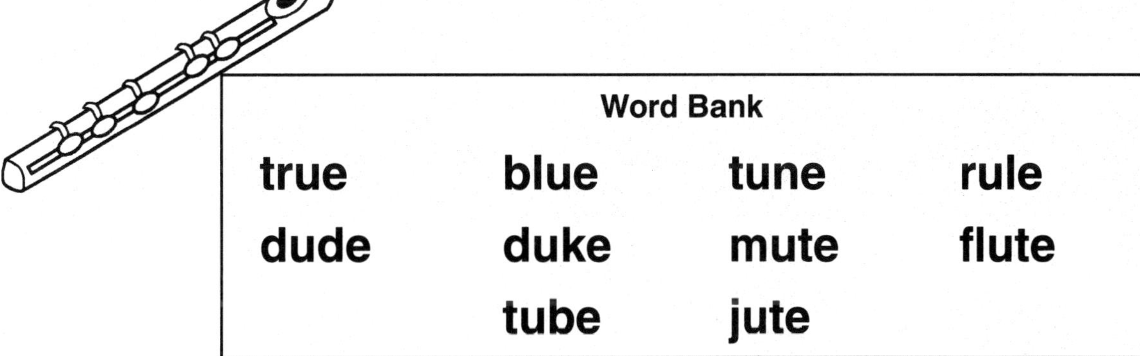

Name____________________________

Unscramble the sentences. Cut out the words and put them in order to make a sentence. Glue the sentences on a separate piece of paper.

1.

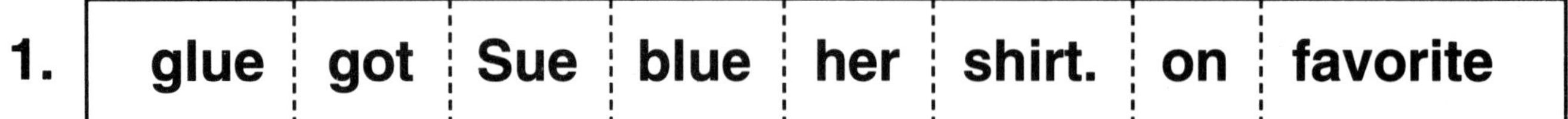

2.

rules?	Do	understand	the	you

3.

park	dude	very	rude.	The	at	was	the

4.

chute.	Tom	his	down	dropped	the	flute

5.

day	The	of	summer	June.	first	in	is

Name______________________________

Write the word that names the picture.

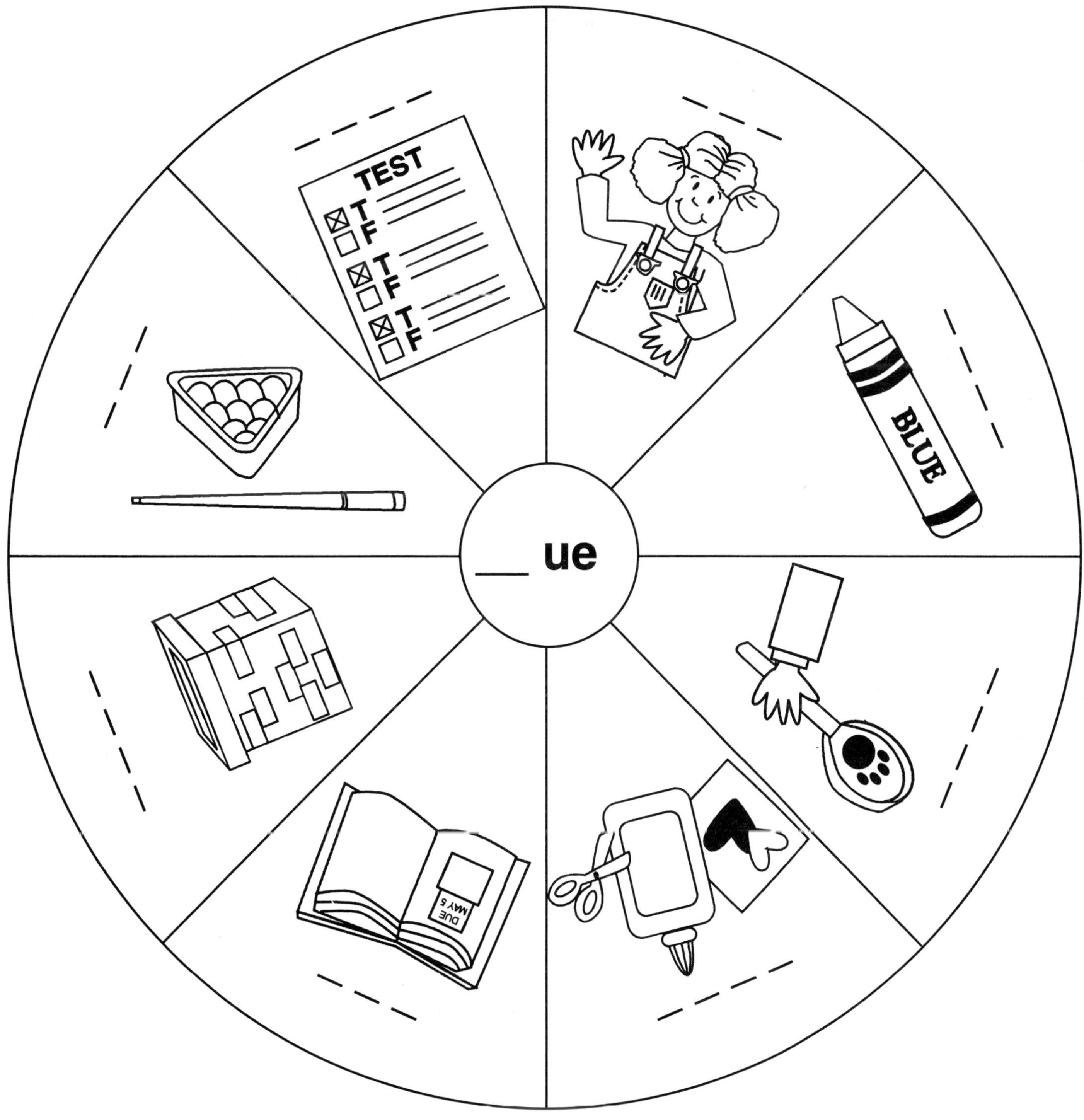

Name________________________

Match the word to its definition. Draw a line from the word to the definition.

1. rude	a. a straight strip used for measuring
2. blue	b. a fruit
3. brute	c. not polite
4. prune	d. a work animal
5. mule	e. a color
6. ruler	f. a mean person

Write a sentence using each word.

1. ____

2. ____

3. ____

4. ____

5. ____

6. ____

Name_______________________

Write 4 words that rhyme.

Name____________________________

Fill in the missing words using the words in the word bank.

1. The last day of school will be __________ 7th.
2. Joe borrowed Anthony's __________ for art.
3. His family took a __________ ride into the Grand Canyon.
4. Jenny practices her __________ every day.
5. Everyone thought she looked __________ in her new dress.
6. She squeezed the toothpaste from a toothpaste __________.
7. The money for the field trip is __________ on Monday.
8. The children sang a __________ as they walked to the park.

Word Bank			
tube	tune	flute	June
due	glue	mule	cute

Name____________________________

Sort the words into 2 groups - nouns and verbs. In some cases a word can be both a noun or a verb. Write those words in both groups.

Naming - Nouns	**Action - Verbs**
______________________	______________________
______________________	______________________
______________________	______________________
______________________	______________________
______________________	______________________
______________________	______________________
______________________	______________________
______________________	______________________
______________________	______________________
______________________	______________________

tube	**due**	**Sue**	**flute**
glue	**ruler**	**prune**	**tune**
	cue	**cube**	

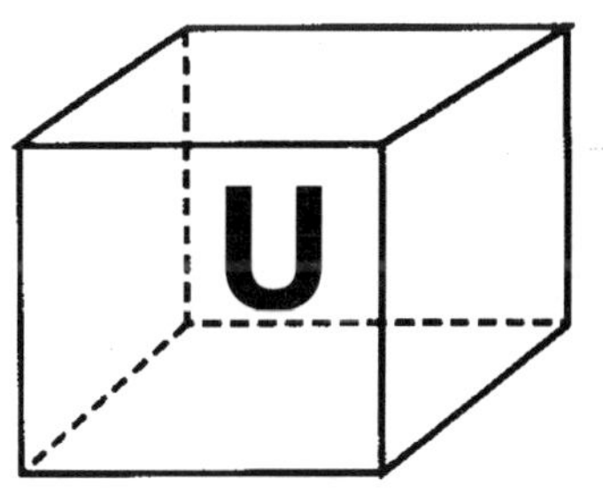

Name_______________________

Memory Game

Cut out the word cards. Mix up the cards and place them face down in 3 rows across and 6 rows down. Play "Memory".

Sue	rude	fuse
jute	prune	glue
tube	duke	cube
Sue	rude	fuse
jute	prune	glue
tube	duke	cube

Word Families

-ace	-ade	-age	-aid	-ail	-ain	-ake
face	fade	cage	laid	fail	lain	bake
lace	blade	page	maid	Gail	main	cake
pace	made	rage	paid	hail	pain	fake
race	wade	sage	raid	jail	rain	Jake
brace	grade	wage	braid	mail	brain	lake
grace	shade	stage		nail	chain	make
place	spade			pail	drain	quake
space	trade			rail	grain	rake
trace				sail	plain	take
				tail	stain	wake
				snail	strain	flake
				trail	train	snake

-ale	-ame	-ate	-ave	-ea	-each	-ead
bale	came	date	cave	pea	beach	bead
dale	fame	fate	Dave	sea	peach	lead
gale	game	gate	gave	tea	reach	read
male	lame	hate	pave	flea	teach	knead
pale	name	Kate	save	plea	bleach	plead
sale	same	late	wave		preach	
tale	tame	rate	brave			
scale	blame	plate	grave			
stale	flame	skate	slave			
whale	shame	state	shave			

-eak	-eal	-ear	-eat	-eed	-eel	-eet
beak	deal	dear	beat	deed	feel	beet
leak	heal	fear	heat	feed	heel	feet
peak	meal	gear	meat	need	keel	meet
teak	real	hear	neat	seed	kneel	greet
weak	seal	near	seat	weed	peel	sheet
creak	teal	rear	cheat	bleed	reel	sleet
freak	squeal	year	pleat	freed	steel	street
sneak	steal	clear	treat	greed	wheel	sweet
speak		smear	wheat	speed		tweet
squeak		spear		tweed		
streak						

Word Families

-ice	-ide	-ight	-ile	-ine	-ite	-ive
dice	hide	knight	file	dine	bite	dive
lice	ride	light	mile	fine	kite	five
mice	side	might	Nile	line	quite	hive
nice	tide	night	pile	mine	rite	jive
rice	wide	right	tile	nine	site	live
vice	bride	sight	smile	pine	white	chive
price	glide	tight	while	vine	write	drive
slice	pride	bright		wine	sprite	strive
twice	slide	flight		shine		thrive
	stride	slight		spine		
				whine		

-oat	-oke	-old	-one	-ope	-ose	-ove
boat	coke	bold	bone	cope	hose	cove
coat	poke	fold	lone	hope	nose	wove
moat	woke	gold	tone	mope	pose	clove
bloat	yoke	hold	zone	pope	rose	drove
goat	broke	mold	clone	rope	chose	grove
float	choke	old	phone	scope	close	stove
throat	smoke	sold	shone	slope	those	
	spoke	told	stone			
	stroke	scold				

-ube	-ude	-ue	-ule	-une	-ute	-use
cube	dude	cue	mule	June	cute	fuse
tube	nude	due	rule	tune	jute	muse
	rude	Sue	yule	prune	lute	ruse
	crude	blue			mute	
	prude	clue			brute	
		flue			flute	
		glue			chute	
		true				